CW01512447

Original title:
Symphony of Souls

Author: Lan Donne
ISBN HARDBACK: 978-1-80560-134-0
ISBN PAPERBACK: 978-1-80560-599-7

Echoes of Each Other

In shadows cast by moonlit shores,
We wander through forgotten doors.
Each heartbeat strikes a timeless chord,
In silence, we are thus adored.

The whispers float on evening air,
Reminders of a love laid bare.
In every glance, a story spun,
Cascading like the setting sun.

Together, we are soft and true,
As echoes dance in shades of blue.
Through laughter's thread, our souls entwine,
In harmony, our hearts align.

From distant shores to realms anew,
We trace the lines of me and you.
In every moment, grace and pain,
Our union, like a sweet refrain.

As stars prepare to grace the night,
We find our paths, dimmed and bright.
In every sigh, a gentle spark,
Two souls, igniting from the dark.

The Harmonious Unfolding

With every step, the rhythm sways,
In twilight hues, we find our ways.
The dance of time, a tender feel,
Each note we play, a truth revealed.

Underneath the vast expanse,
We move together in a trance.
The music flows, a sacred thread,
In whispers soft, our dreams are fed.

From whispered tales of dawn's embrace,
To twilight's kiss, a gentle grace.
We weave our story, line by line,
In every pause, our spirits shine.

In gardens lush, where hopes reside,
We roam the paths where hearts confide.
And as the world begins to fade,
In harmony, our hearts cascade.

So let the symphony unfold,
In colors bright, in shades of gold.
With every chord, we shall ignite,
A lasting love, our purest light.

Whispered Notes of Affinity

In quiet spaces, our hearts hum,
A melody that's soft and warm.
Each whispered note, a secret shared,
In tender tones, we both are bared.

The world around us fades away,
As bonds grow strong, come what may.
In fleeting glances, stories bloom,
Like flowers bursting through the gloom.

With every laugh, a sweet refrain,
Through joy and sorrow, love's domain.
In shadows cast by time's embrace,
We find our own enchanting place.

In quiet nights and starlit dreams,
We dance together, or so it seems.
Through whispered vows beneath the sky,
With every heartbeat, we comply.

So follow where our spirits lead,
In whispered notes, we plant the seed.
In perfect harmony, we strive,
As whispered notes keep love alive.

The Hush Between

In silent woods, whispers roam,
Nature's breath finds its home.
Soft echoes dance through the trees,
Calmness flows with the gentle breeze.

Stars above twinkle and sigh,
The moon watches from the sky.
In these moments, hearts align,
Time stands still, a sacred sign.

Through the night, shadows blend,
Creating paths that never end.
Voices hushed, eyes softly meet,
In stillness, we find our beat.

Nature's hush, a comforting balm,
A soothing peace, forever calm.
In the quiet, we are free,
Embracing all that we can be.

Enchanted Togetherness

Beneath the sky, where dreams take flight,
We hold each other, hearts alight.
In laughter's song, we find our place,
Two souls merging in warm embrace.

Whispers shared in twilight's glow,
Secrets captured, softly flow.
Fingers entwined in a delicate dance,
Lost in the magic of this romance.

Every glance, a story told,
In moments shared, our love unfolds.
A tapestry woven, rich and bright,
Together we shine, day and night.

With every pulse, our spirits rise,
A world created through shared sighs.
In time's embrace, forever we'll stay,
Enchanted together, come what may.

Intersections of Life

Paths converging in a quiet street,
Fates collide where strangers meet.
In the chaos, stories intertwine,
Lives etched together, yours and mine.

Moments flicker like fireflies,
Smiles exchanged, no goodbyes.
A fleeting glance, or a shared cheer,
Building bridges, erasing fear.

In every corner, tales resound,
Lost souls journey, love is found.
Through joys and sorrows, we connect,
In the weave of life, we reflect.

With each choice, paths realign,
In the grand tapestry, we entwine.
Intersections, a dance so profound,
A symphony of lives, beautifully bound.

The Language of Light

In dawn's embrace, the world awakes,
Birdsong spills, the silence breaks.
Sunrise paints the sky so bright,
A canvas filled with pure delight.

Golden rays weave through the trees,
Lighting hearts with gentle ease.
In shadows cast, secrets hide,
Yet in the light, we confide.

Every beam, a whisper clear,
Illuminating all we hold dear.
In flickers and glimmers, truth ignites,
The language of light, in hearts it writes.

As daylight fades, stars ignite,
Guiding dreams into the night.
Through soft glows, our spirits take flight,
In the warmth of love, we find our light.

The Rhythm of Reveries

In twilight's soft embrace, we dream,
Where whispers of the night redeem.
The stars align, a dance of light,
Guiding our souls through endless night.

Each heartbeat carries tales untold,
Of lovers' secrets, brave and bold.
In shadows cast by lunar glow,
We wander paths where longings flow.

With every sigh, the minutes chase,
The pulse of time, a tender grace.
In reveries, our spirits soar,
Beyond the realms of evermore.

Through fleeting moments, memories weave,
A tapestry of what we believe.
In silent pauses, joy arrives,
In rhythm found, our essence thrives.

So let us linger in this place,
Where dreams awaken, hearts embrace.
In the rhythm of our reveries,
Life's melody, a sweet reprise.

Voice of the Collective

In the hush of crowded streets, we hear,
A symphony of voices, crystal clear.
Echoes of hope, dreams intertwined,
The pulse of many hearts aligned.

As footsteps march to rhythms bold,
Stories of struggle and triumph told.
Together we rise, a force so grand,
United we stand, hand in hand.

In shadows cast by doubt and fear,
We share the burdens, the laughter near.
A chorus sung in perfect tune,
Underneath the watchful moon.

Through trials faced and battles worn,
The voice of the many, a new day born.
In unity, our spirits shine,
Creating peace, a sacred line.

So let our voices lift the night,
From whispers soft to soaring flight.
In the heart of the collective beat,
We find our strength, a bond complete.

Unfolding Harmonies

In gentle waves, the music flows,
Through quiet woods where daylight glows.
Each note a whisper, soft and sweet,
Unfolding harmonies, we greet.

The breeze carries tales both old and new,
Nature's song in a dance so true.
With every rustle, leaves confer,
A dialogue profound, a soft stir.

In moments shared, our spirits blend,
With melodies that never end.
In laughter's echoes, joy shall bloom,
Unfolding dreams erase the gloom.

Through valleys deep and mountains high,
The harmonies of life draw nigh.
In every heart, a song resides,
Awakening where love abides.

So let us tune into this grace,
Find solace in each other's space.
In the unfolding, we are free,
Harmonies that set our spirits glee.

Threads of Tranquility

In morning's light, the world awakes,
With gentle sighs, the stillness breaks.
Threads of tranquility weave anew,
In quiet moments just for you.

Soft whispers of the morning breeze,
Embrace the day with tender ease.
Each petal's fall, a calm decree,
In nature's song, we find the key.

Through winding paths where shadows play,
Tranquility guides the heart's ballet.
In every heartbeat, peace resides,
Within the soul where hope abides.

As twilight paints the sky in shades,
Our worries fade, and silence invades.
In tranquil waters, reflections gleam,
Threads of serenity, our dream.

So let us cherish every breath,
The stillness brings a sweet caress.
In life's embrace, we find our way,
Threads of tranquility each day.

The Tapestry of Time

Threads of moments intertwined,
Stitching memories in the mind.
Colors blend, soft and bright,
Creating shadows, weaving light.

Hours slip through fingers fast,
Echoes of the present, past.
Stitches whisper tales untold,
In this tapestry, life unfolds.

Patterns shift with every breath,
Life's design, a dance with death.
Each knot a tale, a fleeting glance,
In the fabric of fate, we dance.

Time's embrace, a gentle hold,
Stories shared, both fierce and bold.
From dawn's light to dusk's embrace,
Each thread finds its destined place.

The loom of life continues to spin,
Crafting futures where dreams begin.
In the tapestry, we find our way,
Binding hearts, come what may.

Murmurs of the Infinite

Whispers echo in the night,
Secrets carried, taking flight.
Stars above, in silence gleam,
Tales unfold within a dream.

Waves of time wash over us,
In the stillness, no need to rush.
Eternal moments softly hum,
In the dark, the shadows come.

Each sound a journey to explore,
Opening vast and whispered doors.
In the depths of quiet space,
Infinite thoughts find their place.

Murmurs rise like misty fog,
Embracing peace, clearing the smog.
Lost in thoughts that twine and weave,
In this stillness, we believe.

Voices from the cosmic sea,
Remind us of what's yet to be.
In the night's soft, gentle sigh,
Murmurs linger, never die.

Interlude of Dreams

In the twilight, dreams take flight,
Whispers painting stars so bright.
Moments linger, softly glide,
In this realm, we lose all pride.

Chasing shadows, fleeting grace,
In the night, we find our place.
Each heartbeat, a secret sigh,
Underneath the vast, dark sky.

Voices echo, stories blend,
In the silence, worlds transcend.
Threads of wishes, softly spun,
As the night begins to run.

Glimmers flash, a fleeting glance,
In the dance of dreams, we prance.
Holding tight to hopes we seek,
In this moment, all is weak.

Yet in weakness, strength we find,
In this realm, hearts intertwined.
As the dawn begins to beam,
We awaken from the dream.

Harmony within the Void

In the void, a whisper sings,
Echoes of forgotten things.
Silent notes begin to weave,
In the dark, we learn to believe.

Stars align in cosmic dance,
Every heartbeat holds a chance.
Within the silence, beauty grows,
In the shadows, a mystery flows.

Harmony in tangled lines,
Woven threads where fate entwines.
Each breath a song of the night,
Lost in dreams, we find our light.

Embrace the stillness, find the peace,
In the void, our hearts release.
With every pause, the world expands,
Harmony flows through unseen hands.

In the depths, a canvas clear,
Painting visions, drawing near.
Within the chaos, sweet resolve,
In this void, our souls evolve.

The Language of Starry Eyes

In twilight's grasp, they softly gleam,
Whispers of hearts in a cosmic dream.
Beneath the veil of a velvet sky,
Silent secrets, they shimmer and sigh.

With every glance, a story told,
Of ancient stars and futures bold.
Caught in the web of a cosmic dance,
Each twinkle a spark, a luminous chance.

Their brilliance paints the night so vast,
Reminders of times that forever last.
Through galaxies wide, they find their way,
Guiding lost souls, come what may.

A universe alive in their gaze,
Journeys unfold in a timeless haze.
Together we drift, in a soft embrace,
In starry eyes, we find our place.

Boundless love in constellations bright,
A language spoken in pure starlight.
Each twinkle a promise, a wish, a sigh,
In the language of starry eyes, we fly.

Serenade of Hidden Depths

In shadows deep, where secrets dwell,
Soft echoes weave a mystic spell.
The heart's refrain, a gentle sigh,
A melody born of the night sky.

In every note, a yearning trace,
For dreams that linger in quiet space.
The moonlit path begins to unfold,
Stories of love, waiting to be told.

Whispers of souls, in silence blend,
Where fears dissolve and hopes transcend.
A serenade sung by the unseen,
In hidden depths, where we have been.

Through depths we wade, in waters clear,
Finding solace in what we hold dear.
The song of life, a symphonic rise,
In the serenade of hidden depths, we fly.

With every heartbeat, a truth becomes,
A tapestry woven with timeless drums.
In this embrace, we find our breath,
In the serenade, we conquer death.

Choreography of Souls in Twilight

In twilight's glow, we sway and spin,
A dance of hearts, where dreams begin.
With every step, our spirits collide,
In the choreography where worlds abide.

Beneath the stars, the rhythm flows,
Bringing to life what no one knows.
A silent pact in the cool night air,
Bound by the movements we both share.

With every twirl, our secrets blend,
In the embrace that will not end.
Love's gentle power, a force divine,
As two souls intersect, we entwine.

Across the dark, the music calls,
In whispered notes, our passion falls.
Each heartbeat echoes, a vibrant tune,
In the choreography under the moon.

Together we twine, through shadow and light,
Sketching our dreams in the still of night.
In this dance, our fears take flight,
Choreography of souls, pure delight.

Interwoven Rhythms of Being

In every heartbeat, a story starts,
Interwoven rhythms echo in our hearts.
Life's tender pulse, a vibrant line,
Each moment shared, a glimpse divine.

Through laughter and tears, we carve our way,
In the fabric of time, where colors sway.
With threads of joy and strands of pain,
We weave together, again and again.

The dance of life, a vibrant thread,
Connecting all, as we forge ahead.
In silence, we speak, in stillness, we find,
Interwoven rhythms, eternally kind.

With each connection, a tale unfolds,
In the tapestry, where life beholds.
We cherish the ties that bind and blend,
In rhythms of being, we transcend.

Together we sway, through fate and chance,
In this grand design, we learn to dance.
Interwoven souls, in harmony sing,
In the beauty of life, our spirits take wing.

Whirlwind of Whispers

In shadows deep, the voices play,
Secrets of night softly sway,
Threads of fear, and threads of hope,
In this dance, we learn to cope.

Whirls of tales, both dark and light,
Carried on breeze, lost from sight,
Echoed dreams that never fade,
In whispers, our fears cascade.

Softly spoken, a tender sigh,
Winds of change, they pass us by,
Through the storm, we find our way,
In every whisper, our hearts sway.

As chaos spins, we hold our ground,
In the silence, solace found,
Voices blend, entwine, and bend,
In this whirlwind, spirits mend.

Let the whispers guide our fate,
In the dusk, we contemplate,
Through the maelstrom of the night,
We emerge, reborn, in light.

Soliloquy of Spirits

In the twilight, shadows talk,
Echoing dreams along the walk,
Spirits linger in silence deep,
Guardians of secrets that we keep.

A gentle breeze, a whispered name,
Each soul dances, ignites the flame,
Binding moments, lost in time,
In this soliloquy, we climb.

Voices tangled in cosmic thread,
Hearts suspended, stories spread,
Through the void, their tales are spun,
An endless journey just begun.

Rising cadence, soft yet strong,
Each spirit sings where they belong,
Melodies of love and pain,
In the echo, we remain.

Let us listen, the wisdom flows,
From every heart, a story grows,
In the silence, truth reveals,
In the whispers, our soul feels.

The Interlacing Melodies

Strings of fate, in harmony,
Every note, a memory,
Chords entwined in twilight's glow,
Tales of life that ebb and flow.

Through the silence, music weaves,
In every heart, a thread that cleaves,
Resonance deep, connection strong,
In this symphony, we belong.

Winds of change, they stir the song,
In the rapture, we all long,
For the moments, sweet and rare,
To embrace the love we share.

Dancing rhythms, time set free,
Crafting dreams in harmony,
With every pulse, our spirits soar,
In the melodies, we explore.

Let the notes caress the night,
Infuse our souls with pure delight,
In this concert of the heart,
Together, we shall never part.

Oracle of the Heart

In quiet corners, visions bloom,
Echoes linger, dispel the gloom,
Whispers of fate, secrets untold,
In the heart, the truth unfolds.

The oracle speaks through silent tears,
Navigating through the years,
Guiding souls with gentle grace,
In the stillness, we find our place.

Pages turning, stories weave,
Intuition helps us believe,
Through shadows, the light will spark,
The oracle's song ignites the dark.

In soft murmurs, we see the light,
Paths illuminated in the night,
Each heartbeat a sacred sign,
Leading us back to what is divine.

As the clock ticks, we draw near,
Embracing moments, shedding fear,
In the heart, wisdom resides,
In the oracle, our truth abides.

The Collective Pulse

In the rhythm of our hearts,
A symphony of voices rise.
Each beat a song of unity,
Echoing beneath the skies.

Through shadows and through light,
We weave our dreams anew.
Together in the silence,
Each spirit's path shines through.

With whispers of the wind,
And laughter in the night,
We dance the dance of ages,
In harmony, our flight.

Threads of gold entwined,
We share a space divine.
In the cadence of our lives,
Collective souls align.

From the depths of our being,
We rise with fervent grace.
In the pulse of existence,
We find our sacred place.

Invitations to Inner Wholeness

In the quiet of the mind,
Invitation to reflect.
Embrace the soft stillness,
In whispers, we connect.

Each thought a gentle breeze,
That stirs the aching soul.
With love's radiant embrace,
We seek to feel made whole.

Unraveling our stories,
With kindness as our guide.
Embracing all the shadows,
Presence by our side.

Unity in fragments,
We gather every part.
With tender hands, we mend,
The fabric of the heart.

Through journeys deep within,
We meet our truest selves.
Invitations softly given,
Where inner peace dwells.

Chants of the Cosmos

In the vastness of the stars,
Chants echo through the night.
Celestial whispers calling,
Guiding each heart's flight.

The universe is singing,
A melody of grace.
Each note a spark of wisdom,
In time and sacred space.

With every pulse of starlight,
We find our sacred song.
In the dance of cosmic energy,
Together, we belong.

Awakened in our spirits,
We rise with voices clear.
Chants of love and beauty,
Across the spheres we steer.

Forever in the rhythm,
Of galaxies that spin.
In the heart of existence,
Our journey shall begin.

The Gathering of Souls

In the circle of our spirits,
We gather hand in hand.
With stories to be shared,
In this sacred land.

Every journey we embrace,
With open hearts and minds.
In the warmth of our connection,
True solace we will find.

Voices whisper in the night,
Carrying our dreams.
Together we are stronger,
Or so it surely seems.

Through laughter and through tears,
We hold each other near.
In the gathering of souls,
We lose and find our cheer.

With every breath a promise,
In unity we rise.
Together through the ages,
Beneath the vast, bright skies.

Whispers of the Spirit

In twilight's glow, a whisper flows,
Through branches swayed, where softness grows.
A gentle voice within the breeze,
Calls forth the heart, invites to freeze.

Echoes of dreams in dusky light,
Reveal the truths that surge from night.
A flicker here, a shadow there,
The spirit dances, light as air.

Upon the stillness, silence falls,
Where nature listens, magic calls.
In quietude, the soul lays bare,
The whispers rise, a solemn prayer.

With every breath, a tale unfolds,
In ancient woods, where time molds.
A symphony of thoughts untold,
In murmurs soft, the heart grows bold.

As night surrenders to dawn's embrace,
The spirit stirs, begins to trace.
A tapestry of life and light,
Whispers of hope in morning's flight.

Tides of Togetherness

In waves that crash upon the shore,
Our hearts align, forevermore.
Together we stand, side by side,
In every challenge, we confide.

The moonlit night, a guiding friend,
Our laughter dances, fears transcend.
With every tide, our bond grows strong,
In harmonious waves, we belong.

Through stormy skies and calm we sail,
Each whispered secret tells the tale.
In gentle currents, love sails free,
A journey shared, just you and me.

The world may change, but we will stay,
With hands entwined, we find our way.
Through shifting sands and ebbing dreams,
Together we are, or so it seems.

In every moment, we create,
A future bright, no room for fate.
In tides of joy and sorrows deep,
Our hearts will hold, our promises keep.

Resonance of Being

In silence deep, a pulse is felt,
The sound of life, where echoes melt.
A symphony of hearts aligns,
In sacred breaths, the spirit shines.

Through every laugh and softened sigh,
Resonance blooms, we cannot lie.
In whispers shared, our truths unfold,
A tapestry of love retold.

With every heartbeat, life we weave,
In moments shared, we must believe.
The harmony of souls combined,
A dance of time, unconfined.

In shadows cast and light embraced,
We journey forth, no steps misplaced.
In every trial, we find our song,
Together, forever, where we belong.

As stars align, and dreams take flight,
A resonance blooms in endless night.
In unity, we rise and sing,
The essence of life, a vibrant ring.

The Dance of Ethereal Voices

In twilight's path, soft voices rise,
A dance of light beneath the skies.
With every note, the spirits twirl,
In shadows deep, their whispers swirl.

From realm to realm, their stories flow,
In melodic waves, the heart shall know.
A cadence bright, in stillness spun,
The dance continues, never done.

In golden hues, the echoes glide,
Through realms unseen, where dreams reside.
With laughter loud and sorrow's tune,
Their essence glows beneath the moon.

In every breath, the voices meld,
The tales of life, in hearts compelled.
Together we sway to their embrace,
A cosmic dance, a sacred space.

With each new dawn, the song renews,
A dance of joy, in morning's hues.
In harmony, forever we sing,
The ethereal voices, life's offering.

Echoes of Eternal Connections

In the stillness of the night,
Whispers travel through the air,
Hearts remember what is right,
Love's embrace, a sacred care.

Time weaves threads both strong and deep,
Each moment a shimmering light,
In memories, we safely keep,
Our souls entwined in endless flight.

Beneath the stars, we find our way,
A chorus sung by ancient trees,
Guiding us through night and day,
In unity, our spirits breeze.

With every heartbeat, life unfolds,
A journey shared, an endless quest,
As stories of the past retold,
In friendship's warmth, we find our rest.

Echoes linger, soft and true,
In realms where shadows dare not dwell,
Together, me and you,
We weave our own eternal spell.

The Dance of Kindred Spirits

Underneath the moon's embrace,
We gather with hearts so free,
In rhythm, we all find our place,
A dance where souls can truly see.

With every step, a silent vow,
To cherish moments, pure and bright,
In laughter shared, in joyful pow,
We twirl beneath the starlit night.

The music plays, a gentle call,
As echoes of the past ignite,
We rise and fall, and sometimes stall,
Yet in this space, there's pure delight.

A connection felt beyond the skin,
In every glance, a spark ignites,
Together, we let the journey spin,
In unity, our spirit flights.

As dawn approaches with its gleam,
We hold the night within our hearts,
For in this dance, we dare to dream,
Kindred spirits, never apart.

Resonance of the Unseen

In silence, echoes softly breathe,
Whispers linger without sound,
A world where thoughts begin to weave,
In realms where magic can be found.

Through shadows where the light is caught,
Invisible, yet always near,
Connections forged in what is sought,
In the heart, our truths adhere.

Beyond the veil, our visions blend,
In unity, they start to bloom,
The love we share will never end,
A garden growing from the gloom.

With every glance, a spark ignites,
Resonance dancing in the air,
In secret places, we find rights,
Unseen bonds we gladly share.

The unseen breadth of life we greet,
In quiet moments, pure and clear,
Resonance echoes at our feet,
In every breath, we want it near.

Tapestry of Unspoken Dreams

In colors bright, our dreams take flight,
Woven together, threads of gold,
In whispered hopes, we find the light,
A story waiting to be told.

Each wish a stitch in life's great seam,
With patience, we craft what we seek,
In every pause, we dare to dream,
In silence soft, our souls will speak.

The tapestry stretches far and wide,
As visions dance within our grasp,
With every heartbeat, we abide,
In this woven time, we clasp.

Through threads of joy and strands of pain,
We gather strength with every tear,
In unity, we'll break the chain,
With dreams that echo, crystal clear.

So here we stand, in hope's embrace,
Together, let us craft our fate,
With every stroke, we find our place,
In this grand weave, we celebrate.

Serenading Shadows

In twilight's gentle embrace, we roam,
Whispers of secrets in the darkened dome.
Flickering lights dance on the trees,
As shadows serenade the evening breeze.

Moonlight cascades on the quiet ground,
In this hushed moment, solace is found.
Stars twinkle softly, a cosmic show,
In the harmony where shadows flow.

Echoes of laughter float through the night,
Memories twine in soft, silver light.
Each pulse of time lingers, a sweet refrain,
In the serenade of night, joy and pain.

Past the horizon, where dreams are spun,
The heart finds rhythm as day is done.
With every breath, the shadows embrace,
In this sacred dance, we find our place.

So let the night wrap us in its veil,
With shadows' whispers, we'll set sail.
Together we'll wander, our spirits in flight,
In the serenade of the beautiful night.

The Harmony Within Silence

In the stillness where echoes fade,
A tranquil space where dreams are laid.
Breath of cosmos, a silent tune,
Whispers of peace beneath the moon.

Tender thoughts weave through the air,
In silent moments, we're laid bare.
Each heartbeat resonates, soft and clear,
In the calm of silence, we draw near.

With every sigh, a secret shared,
In the quiet, our souls are bared.
Wrapped in stillness, time stands still,
In harmony's cradle, we softly fill.

Voices unheard, yet deeply felt,
In the silence, our hearts melt.
Understanding blooms, like flowers bright,
In the gentle embrace of silent night.

So let us dance in this hidden space,
Where silence sings with tender grace.
In the stillness, we find our song,
In harmony's heart, we all belong.

Convergence of Heartstrings

Two paths entwined, a fate revealed,
In the garden of dreams, hearts are healed.
Soft melodies weave through the air,
In this convergence, love lays bare.

Fingers touch in a fleeting glance,
A spark ignites in a timeless dance.
With every heartbeat, a rhythm grows,
In this tapestry, our story flows.

Laughter echoes, like chimes of grace,
In unity's warmth, we find our place.
Moments shared, both fragile and bright,
In convergence, we bathe in light.

Through trials faced, together we stand,
In the harmony of a steady hand.
Threads of trust in the fabric spun,
In this convergence, we are one.

So let the journey lead us along,
In heartstrings' weave, forever strong.
Together we'll write, through joy and tears,
In this convergence, we banish fears.

Cadence of Shared Journeys

In the footsteps of time, we wander wide,
Each path a story, where hearts confide.
With laughter and tears, we chart our course,
In the cadence of journeys, we find our force.

Through sunlit valleys and shadowy hills,
In every moment, adventure spills.
Shared dreams woven in the fabric of fate,
In the rhythm of journeys, we celebrate.

Hand in hand, through trials we stride,
In the dance of life, we'll never hide.
With courage and hope lighting our way,
In the cadence of shared, bright days.

Voices rise in melodies sweet,
Every heartbeat's echo, a beautiful feat.
In harmony, our spirits align,
In the cadence of journeys, hearts entwine.

So let us roam, where paths unfold,
In the tales of love, both new and old.
Together we will write, our story clear,
In the cadence of life, forever near.

Lyrical Threads of Infinity

In the silence, whispers weave,
Stars align, they gently cleave.
Time dances in a fleeting glow,
Hearts entwined, where dreams flow.

Eternal echoes through the night,
Guiding souls with soft moonlight.
Chasing shadows, we ignite,
The fire of moments, pure delight.

With every breath, a story spun,
Under the gaze of the setting sun.
Weaving tales of love and fate,
Resonating in the grand estate.

In cosmic currents, we drift far,
Connected deep, like each bright star.
Threads of laughter, threads of tears,
An endless tapestry through years.

So let us dance in twilight's sigh,
As stardust whispers, never die.
In the weave of galaxies we roam,
Finding in chaos, our true home.

Notes from Beyond

Soft melodies across the breeze,
Carry whispers from the trees.
Each note a fragment, a sacred sign,
Binding worlds, both yours and mine.

Chords of ancient, untold times,
Resounding through the mountains' climbs.
In every silence, music plays,
Opening hearts in myriad ways.

The universe sings in cosmic glee,
Rhythm of life, wild and free.
Countless echoes, a celestial choir,
Fueling the spark of our desire.

Through the ether, vibrations soar,
Weaving connections, forevermore.
A symphony in wounded light,
Guiding us through the darkest night.

In the stillness, we find our groove,
Dancing to chords, we begin to move.
Let the music play, let it blend,
Notes from beyond, our souls we mend.

Pulses of a Cosmic Dream

Whirling galaxies in cosmic dance,
Every heartbeat, a fleeting chance.
Starlit whispers in the vast unknown,
Fragments of dreams, seeds we've sown.

With every breath, a universe spins,
Tales of loss, where love begins.
Orbiting thoughts, in silence, they grow,
Pulsing rhythms, a gentle flow.

In the tapestry of night and day,
We forge connections, come what may.
Time a river flowing free,
Carving paths to eternity.

Floating gently on stardust streams,
Awakening from our cosmic dreams.
Navigating through the glowing streams,
We find ourselves in ancient themes.

Every pulse a spark ignites,
Carrying hope through darkest nights.
In the cosmos, our spirits gleam,
United in this endless dream.

The Musicality of Our Encounters

In fleeting moments, melodies arise,
Intertwining like the stars in skies.
Harmonic laughter, whispers sweet,
Each glance a note, a rhythmic beat.

Strumming heartstrings, tender and true,
Every exchange, a vibrant hue.
Dancing together, we create a song,
In the tempo of life, where we belong.

Echoes of joy in every embrace,
Chords of memories, time can't erase.
From laughter's spark to tears that flow,
The musicality of love we sow.

As seasons change, our rhythm evolves,
In the symphony, our soul resolves.
Every encounter, a precious note,
In the grand score, we freely float.

So let us sing in perfect harmony,
A duet woven through destiny.
In the cadence of life, we find our way,
A timeless song, come what may.

Harmonies of the Heart

In quiet moments, love does swell,
A gentle whisper, a secret spell.
Like rivers flowing, deep and wide,
Two souls entwined, no need to hide.

Soft laughter dances in the air,
With every glance, a silent prayer.
The joy of knowing, hand in hand,
Together forever, a timeless band.

In shadows long and sunlight fair,
Hearts beat close, a bond to share.
Through trials faced, through joys we roam,
In every heartbeat, we find our home.

The stars above, they sing our song,
In perfect harmony, where we belong.
With every tear and every smile,
We weave a tapestry, mile by mile.

Across the skies, our dreams take flight,
In the embrace of the soft, moonlight.
Through every season, hope imparts,
A life composed of harmonies, hearts.

Echoes of Existence

In the stillness, whispers grow,
Footsteps tread where shadows flow.
Moments linger, time stands still,
In echoes deep, we find our will.

The sun dips low, the sky ignites,
As day surrenders to starry nights.
Within the silence, secrets bloom,
In every corner of this room.

Memory dances on fleeting breath,
Carrying stories from life to death.
Voices call from ages past,
In echoes of love, their shadows cast.

The sands of time slip through our hands,
Yet in our hearts, forever stands.
A fragile thread, we weave with care,
In existence shared, we find our prayer.

Awake in dreams where futures blend,
With every heartbeat, we transcend.
In the rhythm of life, we find our song,
Echoes of existence, we all belong.

Melodies in the Mist

As dawn awakens with soft embrace,
In layers of mist, a magic space.
Whispers of morning, so light and sweet,
In nature's symphony, hearts skip a beat.

The rustling leaves sing gentle tunes,
While shadows dance beneath the moons.
Each note carried on a breath of air,
Invokes a longing, a silent prayer.

Through veils of fog, the world transforms,
In melodies soft, the spirit warms.
Embracing moments, fleeting, rare,
A harmony born from love and care.

The river hums a timeless refrain,
As life flows onward, joy and pain.
In every heartbeat, we find desire,
Melodies rise, lifting us higher.

In twilight's haze, the stars align,
With whispered secrets, hearts intertwine.
In the embrace of eternity's bliss,
We dance to the rhythm of misty kiss.

Chords of Connection

With every glance, a spark ignites,
Binding our souls, oh such delights.
In laughter shared, and stories told,
We weave a tapestry of threads of gold.

The world spins wildly, yet we find peace,
In chords of connection, love will increase.
Through valleys low, or mountains high,
Together we soar, learning to fly.

In silence spoken, in looks exchanged,
A heart's communication, beautifully arranged.
Through paths diverse, our journey's made,
With every step, fears start to fade.

Feel the rhythm as time goes by,
With every heartbeat, a soft, sweet sigh.
In waves of emotion, we rise and fall,
In chords of connection, we find it all.

So let us cherish this sacred bond,
In every moment, of which we are fond.
Through love's embrace, we shall remain,
Chords of connection, joy and pain.

Harmonies of the Heart

In the quiet of the night,
Whispers float upon the breeze.
Every heartbeat sings a tune,
Bathed in love that never flees.

Strings of fate entwine us close,
Dancing in the softest light.
Each glance a note, a gentle touch,
Creating music in the night.

With every breath, our souls align,
Resonating deep within.
Together we compose a song,
An opus born from where we've been.

Time may fade, but we will stay,
In harmony, forever strong.
Through the trials and tender joys,
Our rhythms pulse, we can't go wrong.

So let us hold this symphony,
The world will melt away in bliss.
For when our voices intertwine,
There lies a magic in each kiss.

Celestial Echoes

Stars alight with stories old,
Whispers woven through the skies.
In each twinkle, secrets unfold,
In silence, the universe sighs.

Moonbeams dance on endless nights,
Painting dreams from shadows cast.
Constellations guide our flights,
Echoes of the cosmic vast.

Galaxies swirl in deep embrace,
A symphony of light and dark.
Through the void, we find our place,
In every glow, a lasting spark.

Celestial songs, in harmony,
Reach out, pulling at our hearts.
In every note, we are set free,
In the cosmos, no one departs.

Let us listen, let us feel,
The echoes of the stars above.
In their beauty, we reveal,
A boundless, everlasting love.

Whispered Chords of Existence

In the fabric of the day,
Threads of sounds brush past our ears.
Life's soft music leads the way,
A melody beyond our fears.

Gentle breezes tell their tales,
Rustling leaves, a sweet refrain.
Nature's rhythm never fails,
Awakening the heart again.

Moments draped in harmony,
Every laugh a crystal tone.
In the stillness, we can see,
The beauty of the life we've sown.

Each heartbeat strikes a subtle chord,
Resounding through our fleeting time.
In this dance, we are adored,
Our spirits blend, a perfect rhyme.

Through the whispers, life will sing,
Binding us in sacred grace.
Together, we are everything,
In this vast, embracing space.

Melodies in the Moonlight

Beneath the moon's enchanting gaze,
Silence weaves a silver thread.
In the night, our hearts ablaze,
With every word, our spirits spread.

Whispers float on misty air,
Stars become our urgent muse.
In this realm, we have no care,
For in the dark, we cannot lose.

Echoed laughter guides us close,
Painting shadows in the night.
Wrapped in starlight, we morose,
In every touch, a spark ignites.

The world's asleep, but we awake,
Crafting dreams in tender light.
In this moment, we partake,
A serenade that feels so right.

So let the moonlight be our guide,
In this melody, we find peace.
With every note, our hearts collide,
As time dissolves, our love won't cease.

The Echoing Silence

In quiet rooms where shadows play,
The whispers of the thoughts convey.
Each pause a sound, each breath a tune,
In the stillness, hearts commune.

Echoes dance in empty air,
Memories linger, sweet and rare.
Silence sings its solemn song,
A gentle place where dreams belong.

The ticking clock, a distant beat,
In solitude, our souls they greet.
Each heartbeat echoes in the void,
In the silence, love's deployed.

Through the night, the stars will gleam,
As silence wraps us like a dream.
In the hush, the world feels wide,
In the stillness, we confide.

Listen close, the quiet speaks,
In the silence, wisdom seeks.
An echo of what once was bright,
In silent moments, we find light.

Unity in Dissonance

In the chaos, we find our way,
Voices clash, yet still we stay.
Harmony lurks in the strife,
A dance of shadows, a song of life.

Different tones, a vibrant blend,
Where disarray and hope extend.
In every note, a story told,
In discord's arms, our dreams unfold.

Together we rise, despite the noise,
In every clash, we hear our joys.
Amidst the storm, we stand steadfast,
Unity forged through contrast vast.

Each battle fought, a lesson learned,
As hearts collide, our passions burned.
In every fight, a chance to see,
The beauty in our diversity.

In the ruckus, love finds space,
In dissonance, we find our place.
Together we sing, through thick and thin,
A symphony where all can win.

Chiming of the Celestial Wind

Beneath the vast and starlit sky,
The winds of change begin to sigh.
Whispers of galaxies far and wide,
In their embrace, our spirits glide.

Stars collide in a graceful dance,
Their cosmic chords, a timeless chance.
In every breath, a universe sings,
In the harmony that the stardust brings.

Moonlit paths where dreams may roam,
Through solar breezes, we find our home.
In the twilight, the heavens chime,
A melody that transcends time.

Celestial winds, they softly call,
In their embrace, we rise, we fall.
Under twilight's watchful eye,
We feel the pulse of the night sky.

With every gust, new stories soar,
In the wind's arms, we are restored.
As stardust dances, hearts entwined,
In the wind's song, we become aligned.

Cadence of Creation

In the silence before the dawn,
Ideas swirl, a new day drawn.
With every thought, the canvas waits,
As visions form through open gates.

Here in this space, the magic brews,
Colors burst, and life renews.
Each heartbeat drums a steady pace,
The rhythm of time in this sacred place.

From chaos born, a plan does take,
A symphony builds, no chance to break.
In every pause, a chance to see,
The art of life, wild and free.

Crafting dreams from whispered air,
Each creation, a love laid bare.
In the rhythm of hands that weave,
A world awakens, hearts believe.

In the cadence of each heartbeat's thrall,
Together we rise, together we fall.
In this dance of dreams we find,
The essence of all humankind.

Unison of Unseen Forces

In shadows deep where whispers play,
The echoes dance in twilight's sway.
With every breath, the silence speaks,
A symphony the heart still seeks.

Through tangled roots, the stories weave,
Of ancient dreams that dare believe.
In hidden paths where starlight glows,
The unseen pulls, the spirit flows.

In every heartbeat, secrets dance,
In quiet moments, fate's romance.
The unseen ties, a gentle thread,
Connecting all, where souls are led.

In unity, the forces blend,
In harmony, beginnings mend.
Like rivers merging, strong and bold,
The tale of life silently told.

Through whispered winds, the journey starts,
In unison, we share our hearts.
An unseen force, a guiding light,
Together soaring into the night.

Lullabies of the Lost

In twilight's grip, the shadows sigh,
A lullaby for those who fly.
The dreams once bright now flicker dim,
In quiet tones, the haunting hymn.

The memories drift on softest air,
A gentle touch, a whispered care.
Through veils of time, their stories glide,
In silence held, they still abide.

Restless souls in moonlight roam,
A journey far away from home.
With every note, their hearts set free,
A serenade to what will be.

In darkest nights, the stars will sing,
Of love and loss, the pain they bring.
For every tear, a tune is spun,
A melody for everyone.

In twilight's arms, we find our peace,
As lullabies of lost souls cease.
With every breath, their love stays near,
A soothing song, forever clear.

Rhythms of Remembrance

In every heartbeat, echoes play,
The rhythms dance in soft ballet.
With every step, a story told,
In vibrant hues, the past unfolds.

Through whispered winds, the tales arise,
Of laughter lost, of silent cries.
In shadows cast, the memories gleam,
A vivid thread, a woven dream.

As time flows on, the spirits glide,
In sacred spaces, they abide.
With every pulse, they intertwine,
In sacred circles, hearts align.

The world may change, yet still we know,
The rhythms of the heart will flow.
In harmony, the past retains,
The echoes heard, the love remains.

In every moment, find the beat,
In rhythms soft, our lives complete.
For in remembrance, we are bound,
In timeless dance, forever found.

Convergence of Hearts

When paths collide, the hearts awake,
With every glance, the bond we make.
In tender moments shared as one,
A masterpiece, our journey spun.

In laughter's glow, in silence deep,
Together now, our promises keep.
Through trials faced, we stand as words,
Like anchored ships in storms of birds.

With every heartbeat, rhythms flow,
In unity, the seeds we sow.
Through all the chaos, love will guide,
In convergence strong, we'll turn the tide.

In whispered dreams, the future glows,
As rivers meet, the current knows.
The tapestry of hearts expands,
In woven strength, together stands.

So let us walk this path as one,
In laughter, tears, and love outrun.
For every moment shared shall be,
A testament of you and me.

The Orchestra of Existence

In the hall where echoes thrive,
Resonance of souls come alive.
Each note a whisper, soft and clear,
A symphony played for all to hear.

Waves of sound, like rivers flow,
Carving paths where hearts will go.
In every silence, a secret told,
An orchestra of dreams, bold and old.

Strings plucked with a delicate grace,
In the dance of time, they find their place.
Woodwinds murmur tales untold,
In colors of night and shades of gold.

Percussion beats in heart's delight,
Marking the passage from day to night.
As harmony weaves through the air,
Existence sings, laying emotions bare.

Together they play, a cosmic chord,
Life's journey, a melody adored.
In every heartbeat, music's born,
An orchestra of existence, never worn.

Celestial Dialogues

Stars converse in the velvet sky,
Whispers of time where dreams undy.
Constellations dance, a cosmic show,
In the silence, their secrets flow.

Planets spin with graceful ease,
Murmurs of love in the cosmic breeze.
Galaxies twirl, a timeless waltz,
In the abyss, there's no fault.

Moonlight bathes the world below,
Questions linger, answers slow.
Stardust sprinkles on earth's face,
Celestial dialogues in endless space.

Hearts align with the twinkling night,
Mysteries shared in soft twilight.
Echoes of laughter up above,
In every setup, shadows of love.

Dinner with comets, laughter with suns,
Celestial tales when day is done.
In the universe, unity reigns,
Dialogues eternal, beyond life's chains.

Strings of Serenity

Gentle hands on taut strings play,
Each stroke a wish, a hope on display.
Harmony flows, a river's grace,
In every note, we find our place.

Breezes hum along the way,
As strings of serenity softly sway.
Plucked with care, they sing their tune,
Echoing hearts beneath the moon.

In the quiet, melodies weave,
Threads of peace, we dare to believe.
With every chord, tensions release,
A balm for spirits, a moment of peace.

Resonating in the depths of night,
Strings vibrating from the sheer delight.
In the orchestra of calm we find,
A serenade that soothes the mind.

Together we create, hearts entwined,
Strings of serenity, a treasure defined.
In simple chords, a world anew,
Bridges of harmony connecting me and you.

Voyage of Vibrations

Embarking on waves of sound so free,
A journey begins, just you and me.
Each pulse a story, every beat a call,
In this voyage of vibrations, we fall.

Whispers of time beneath the skin,
Every note a marker as we spin.
Together we float on this sea of sighs,
Riding the rhythm where freedom lies.

Basslines ground us, a steady beat,
While treble dances lightly on our feet.
With every sway, we're pulled apart,
Vibrations weaving through the heart.

Chords collide, then softly merge,
In this symphony, emotions surge.
A voyage of sound, we set our sail,
In the winds of melody, we will prevail.

As echoes fade into night's embrace,
We trace the vibrations, a sacred space.
With every encounter, our souls align,
In the journey of music, divinely entwined.

Symphonic Revelations of the Heart

In the silence, hearts do sing,
Notes of longing softly ring.
Dreams awaken, spirits soar,
Love's revelation evermore.

Whispers lace through twilight's air,
Melodies of love and care.
Strings of fate entwine so bright,
Guiding souls through the night.

Every heartbeat, a gentle tune,
Harmony beneath the moon.
The symphony of life we hear,
Echoes drawing us near.

Dancing shadows play the score,
Each refrain opens a door.
In this cadence, we find peace,
In the sound, our worries cease.

So let love's music fill the space,
In every note, a warm embrace.
Symphonic revelations start,
Unveiling truths within the heart.

Vibrations of Life's Embrace

Through the ages, life's pulse flows,
In each touch, the spirit knows.
Vibrations dance on gentle tides,
Carries dreams where hope abides.

Colors swirl in morning light,
Every heartbeat feels so right.
The embrace of life surrounds,
Happiness in every sound.

Nature's song, a timeless call,
In unity, we rise, we fall.
Find the rhythm, play your part,
In this dance, we share the heart.

Moments fleeting, yet so sweet,
In each laughter, love's heartbeat.
Life's embrace, both soft and strong,
Guiding us, where we belong.

So let the vibrations intertwine,
Binding souls in love's design.
In every breath, a song we raise,
Living life in vibrant ways.

The Chorus of Togetherness

In the gathering of the kind,
Voices blend, our hearts aligned.
A chorus rich with every tone,
Together, we have always grown.

Threads of laughter weave our days,
In this chorus, love displays.
Harmonies of trust and care,
United souls beyond compare.

Through trials faced and joys embraced,
In each chapter, love is traced.
The melody of friendship true,
Together, we'll make it through.

Each note echoes, a timeless start,
Celebrating the beating heart.
In the dance of life, we twine,
In this chorus, spirits shine.

So hand in hand, we sing as one,
A symphony, our hearts have spun.
In togetherness, forever blessed,
With love's song, we find our rest.

Melodic Whispers Through Time

Whispers float on evening air,
Melodies of dreams laid bare.
Times forgotten, tales retold,
In each note, our stories unfold.

Memories dance on silver streams,
Intertwined with fragile dreams.
Echoes of the past arrive,
In the music, we revive.

Notes of longing sweetly play,
Guiding travelers on their way.
Through the ages, our souls glide,
In this rhythm, we abide.

Stardust falls, the night ignites,
In harmony, we reach new heights.
Moments captured in time's embrace,
Melodic whispers find their place.

With every chord, a voyage starts,
Binding souls, connecting hearts.
Through melodic whispers we find,
The essence of our shared mind.

Embrace of Unique Echoes

In twilight's gentle glow, we find,
Whispers dancing, intertwining,
Each echo, a tale of hearts entwined,
In shadows deep, their song defining.

Through valleys wide, the voices blend,
Like rivers flowing, free and bold,
Unique in each note, they ascend,
A harmony of stories told.

The laughter we share, the tears we shed,
In every moment, memories sway,
A tapestry of words unsaid,
In silent spaces, they find their way.

Among the stars, bright dreams ignite,
A promise wrapped in stardust's weave,
In the embrace of the soft night,
We gather echoes, and we believe.

So let us dance beneath the moon,
With each step, create our song,
For in the night, we'll find our tune,
In unique echoes, we belong.

The Song of the Silent

In the corners where shadows lie,
Silence speaks in tender tones,
With every breath, a soft sigh,
The heart hums in muted zones.

Unseen melodies fill the air,
A lullaby for those awake,
Whispers linger, rich and rare,
In stillness, we feel the ache.

The calm between the vibrant notes,
Each pause a canvas waiting wide,
Where the unvoiced dreamer gloats,
In quietude, we choose to glide.

Amid the noise, we find reprieve,
A sanctuary built with grace,
In silence, we dare to believe,
The hidden song in every space.

So let us cherish silent streams,
Where the unseen finds its way,
For in the hush, there lie our dreams,
In the song of the silent, we sway.

Gathering Rhythms

As dawn unfolds with gentle hands,
The world awakens with a beat,
In every heartbeat, nature stands,
A symphony beneath our feet.

With every step, we find our way,
Through melodies that softly call,
In unity, we sway and play,
A gathering of rhythms, we enthrall.

The rustling leaves, a chorus sweet,
The babbling brook adds its refrain,
In every corner, life's heartbeat,
A dance of joys, a blend of pain.

Let's gather near the crackling fire,
With stories shared and laughter bright,
In rhythm's pulse, our hearts conspire,
To celebrate the fleeting light.

Together in this vital song,
We move as one, in sync, in time,
In gathering rhythms, we belong,
A dance of lives, a perfect rhyme.

The Fabric of Frequencies

In the loom of space and time,
Frequencies weave their silent thread,
A tapestry of love's sweet rhyme,
In every moment, softly spread.

Each pulse and beat, a color bold,
Vibrations dance across the sky,
A fabric rich, with stories told,
In every note, a reason why.

As heartstrings resonate with grace,
The echoes flutter, rise, and fall,
A woven song in every place,
In the silence, we hear it all.

Let's listen close to nature's weave,
In every rustle, wave, and breeze,
For in the sound, we can believe,
The fabric hums, our hearts at ease.

So gather round this vibrant cloth,
In unity, our spirits soar,
The fabric of frequencies, in swath,
A connection felt forevermore.

The Crescendo of Kinship

In whispers soft, our hearts align,
Together we weave a sacred sign.
Through trials faced, we rise and stand,
In love's embrace, we hold each hand.

United voices blend in song,
In every note, we all belong.
With laughter bright, we light the way,
In kinship's grace, we greet each day.

Through stormy seas, our bond remains,
In joy and grief, through all the pains.
Together we dance, like waves to shore,
In harmony's call, we are much more.

Each step we take, a choice to make,
In every heartbeat, love won't break.
With shared dreams, we will explore,
The crescendo of kinship, forevermore.

Spheres of Sound

In whispered tones, the echoes play,
A symphony that guides the way.
Waves of laughter, soft and sweet,
In harmony, our hearts will meet.

Like raindrops dancing on the ground,
Each moment sings, a joy profound.
In every note, a story flows,
A tapestry of sound that grows.

Resonating through the air,
Connecting souls, a bond so rare.
In rhythms shared, we'll find our voice,
Together in the sound, rejoice.

With every chord, our spirits rise,
In layered tones, love never dies.
Spheres of sound, we twirl and spin,
A melody of life within.

Poetry of Perseverance

Through darkest nights, the embers glow,
In whispered strength, the courage flows.
With every line, a story told,
In verses deep, our dreams unfold.

The path may twist, the road may turn,
In every setback, we will learn.
With hope as ink, we write our fate,
In every struggle, we create.

Lines of strength inked on the page,
In every heart, we break the cage.
With passion fierce, we choose to rise,
In the poetry, we reach for skies.

Through storms we march, unwavering,
In steadfast grace, our souls are singing.
The verses pulse, a heartbeat strong,
In perseverance, we belong.

A Ballet of Echoes

In graceful form, the dancers glide,
Through every movement, love and pride.
With whispers soft, their stories weave,
In echoes bright, the heart believes.

The stage alight with dreams and fears,
In every leap, the soul endears.
With rhythms twined, a sweet embrace,
In every twirl, we find our place.

A ballet spun from hope and grace,
In every note, we find our space.
Through shadows cast, they rise anew,
In echoes' dance, the world they view.

With gentle hearts, they share their light,
In every spin, the stars ignite.
A ballet of echoes, pure and free,
In every movement, we are we.

The Pulse of Togetherness

In the heart, we gather close,
Threads of love, our common prose.
In laughter shared and silence found,
Our spirit's dance, a joy profound.

Hand in hand through trials we tread,
With whispered hopes, where dreams are fed.
In every heartbeat, we resonate,
Together strong, we celebrate.

Across the miles, our voices blend,
Moments cherished, time can't suspend.
In unity's glow, shadows fade,
With every step, new joys are made.

Through the storms, we rise as one,
Facing fears 'til the battle's won.
In the embrace of warmth and light,
Together, we reclaim the night.

We'll weave our dreams, a vibrant hue,
With every pulse, a bond that's true.
In the fabric of life, intertwined,
The pulse of us will ever shine.

A Chorus of Convergence

In the stillness, voices rise,
Echoes dance beneath the skies.
Different paths, yet here we stand,
A chorus formed, hand in hand.

Melodies of vibrant tales,
In connection, our spirit sails.
Every note a heartbeat's trace,
Creating harmony in space.

From every corner, colors blend,
As bridges built extend, my friend.
In the symphony of dreams, we sway,
Crafting magic in the fray.

With laughter bright and voices bold,
Our shared reflections weave the gold.
A gathering where stories flow,
Each moment cherished, seeds we sow.

Together we sing, never alone,
In every heart, a sacred tone.
In our convergence, light ignites,
A chorus strong, reaching heights.

The Interwoven Paths

Along the paths where shadows play,
Threads of fate intertwine our way.
In every twist, a tale unfolds,
Stories whispered, forever told.

With every step, a choice is made,
In the fabric of life, dreams cascade.
Journey shared through joy and strife,
In the weft and weave of life.

Through valleys deep and mountains high,
With courage fierce, we learn to fly.
Each intersection, a chance to grow,
In the dance of life, we ebb and flow.

Echoes of laughter, threads of pain,
In the interwoven, there's much to gain.
Together we tread, hand in hand,
In our unity, we take a stand.

As paths converge beneath the stars,
We heal the wounds, erase the scars.
In every heartbeat, love will steer,
The interwoven paths, forever near.

Notes from the Beyond

From the silence, whispers arise,
Echoing truths beyond the skies.
Notes from realms we cannot see,
Messages shared, setting us free.

In the twilight, a soft refrain,
Reminders of love that will remain.
In shadows cast, light finds a way,
Guiding our journey, day by day.

With every heartbeat, wisdom flows,
In the depth, the spirit knows.
Notes from the beyond softly call,
Encouraging us to rise and not fall.

In the moments when we feel lost,
These gentle nudges show us the cost.
Connecting hearts through time and space,
In the notes we find our place.

As we listen to the subtle sound,
In the quiet, our truth is found.
With every note, a bond grows strong,
From the beyond, we all belong.

Chronicles of Connection

In whispers shared beneath the stars,
Two souls align, no matter the scars.
Every heartbeat tells a tale,
Of bonds unbroken, love's soft sail.

Through laughter loud and silence deep,
A tapestry of memories we keep.
In moments fleeting, time stands still,
Connection flows, an endless thrill.

Across the distance, hearts will find,
A way to speak, to intertwine.
Across the realms where echoes play,
Chronicles bloom in light of day.

Embraced by shadows, light will gleam,
In unity, we dare to dream.
With every step, our spirits soar,
In the chronicles, we seek for more.

In laughter's echo and sighs' retreat,
Together we rise, together we meet.
An endless journey, we share as one,
In chronicles woven, never undone.

The Aura of Affection

In gentle glances, warmth ignites,
An aura wrapped in soft delights.
Every touch, a silent vow,
In tender moments, here and now.

Through fragile days and nights so bold,
Affection blooms, a story told.
In every heartbeat, love's embrace,
The aura glows—a sacred space.

With laughter bright or shadows cast,
Together we cherish each moment passed.
In glimmers shared, the world feels bright,
The aura whispers, love's pure light.

Through trials faced, we hold on tight,
In the storm's eye, we seek the light.
The aura of affection flows,
In every challenge, our strength grows.

In whispered dreams and tender sighs,
A radiant bond that never dies.
With every heartbeat, we're intertwined,
In the aura, true love we find.

Song of the Shared Journey

In footsteps traced on sandy shores,
We weave a song that ever soars.
With every twist and turn we take,
A melody for our hearts to make.

Through mountains high and valleys low,
We share the highs, embrace the woe.
In laughter's echo, sorrows fade,
Together, love's sweet serenade.

In whispers soft beneath the moon,
We hum the notes, a gentle tune.
With every note, our spirits rise,
In harmony, we touch the skies.

Through seasons' change, the song remains,
In joyful hearts, love's refrain gains.
With every chord, our souls entwine,
In the song of change, forever shine.

As time unfolds, our symphony grows,
In every heartstring, the melody flows.
With you beside me, I'll always sing,
The song of our spirit, forever in spring.

Crescendo of Compassion

In quiet moments, kindness stirs,
A flame ignites, a heart that purrs.
In gentle hands, we find our way,
Compassion blooms, brightening the day.

Through trials faced and burdens shared,
In every struggle, we show we cared.
A whispered word, a knowing glance,
In the crescendo, love finds its dance.

With arms wide open, hearts embrace,
In fragile times, we find our place.
The rhythm grows, the spirits rise,
Compassion's song, a sweet surprise.

Through every tear and every smile,
We walk together, mile by mile.
In harmony, our souls unite,
In the crescendo, purest light.

With every heartbeat, warmth we share,
In kindness given, we show we care.
In crescendos felt, love will expand,
Compassion's power, hand in hand.

Pathways of Perception

Beyond the trees where shadows play,
Each step we take paves a new way.
With whispers soft and truths laid bare,
We find ourselves in open air.

The road ahead is dimly lit,
Each turn a dance, a spark, a split.
Through winding paths of thought and dream,
We question all, we find our theme.

In echoes past, we hear the call,
A gentle pull, a fiery squall.
With every choice, our spirits soar,
Discovering what we seek and more.

A tapestry of minds entwined,
In every step, new truths we find.
The journey's shape is ours to make,
Through every breath and each heartache.

So walk with me on storied ground,
In every sight, connection found.
As pathways merge, we chart the course,
In pathways of perception, we find force.

The Harmony of Hearts Alight

In the stillness of the night,
Our hearts ignite with warm delight.
With every beat, a chord we play,
Entwined in love, we find our way.

Underneath the starry skies,
A symphony where silence lies.
With gentle hands and tender grace,
We weave our dreams in shared embrace.

Our laughter rings like silver bells,
Creating magic, casting spells.
Through trials faced, together strong,
In harmony, we both belong.

Each whispered word, a note of peace,
In this dance, our fears release.
The melody of hearts, so bright,
In every glance, our souls take flight.

With every dawn, our spirits rise,
In sacred bond, we share the skies.
In love's embrace, we find the light,
The harmony of hearts alight.

Mystic Harmonies

In twilight's glow, the shadows weave,
A tapestry of dreams, believe.
With every breath, a story spun,
In mystic harmonies, we run.

The whispers of the ancient trees,
Unlock their secrets in the breeze.
With every rustle, every sound,
The universe in us is found.

The dance of stars in velvet skies,
Illuminates our souls, they rise.
As echoes fade, we find our voice,
In silken threads of fate, rejoice.

Through labyrinths where shadows blend,
The heart's true rhythm has no end.
In every pulse, we spark the flame,
In mystic harmonies, we name.

So let the waves of night opine,
As dreams and stars in balance shine.
In every moment, let us prance,
In mystic harmonies, take a chance.

The Connection of Currents

Beneath the surface, currents flow,
A dance unseen, where visions grow.
Together, we ride waves of thought,
In every tide, a lesson taught.

The rivers twist, a winding path,
In every ebb, we find the math.
With nature's pulse, we sync our beats,
In flows of love, our journey meets.

In stillness deep, our hearts align,
Through gentle waves, a space divine.
The whispers of the water's song,
Remind us here is where we belong.

Through storms we find our strength anew,
In torrents wild, we birth the blue.
As currents shift, we hold the line,
In connection's depth, we will shine.

So ride the waves, embrace the change,
In every current, life's sweet exchange.
With open hearts, let us explore,
The connection of currents, and more.

The Heart's Resonant Chime

In silence, whispers softly play,
A melody of the heart's sway.
Each beat a note, pure and bright,
Echoing love into the night.

In every pause, a breath that sighs,
Living dreams in tender ties.
From shadows deep, the light ascends,
A score of warmth that never bends.

With every touch, a symphony,
Awakening deep harmony.
The pulse, a song that won't depart,
Each chime a bridge between our hearts.

Through laughter shared and sorrows weep,
A resonance the soul can keep.
In rhythms sweet, together we find,
The music played within our mind.

For in this dance, our spirits soar,
A chime that echoes evermore.
In love's embrace, we truly shine,
Forever held by heart's design.

Orbit of Emotions

In the vast space of dreaming skies,
Feelings spin where starlight lies.
A dance of shadows, bright and dim,
Each orbit pulls, each gravity whim.

Joy flutters close like a sunlit star,
While sorrow circles, hidden afar.
In silence, echoes softly beam,
Uniting hearts in a timeless dream.

Passion burns like a comet's blaze,
While fear rests still in the darkened haze.
Hope twinkles gently, guiding our way,
As emotions swirl in a cosmic play.

The heart's compass, true and strong,
Navigates paths where we belong.
Through every pulse, the universe chimes,
In this orbit of shifting times.

Each feeling leads, a guiding light,
Through planets lost, through endless night.
An astral song where dreams are spun,
Together we rise, forever as one.

Voices in the Twilight

In twilight's hush where shadows creep,
Voices linger, secrets keep.
Whispers blend with evening's sigh,
As day and night together lie.

A serenade of fading light,
Calls to hearts now taking flight.
Memories drift on the cool, soft breeze,
Carrying tales of love that tease.

Each note trembles with the dusk's embrace,
In quietude, we find our place.
The world slows down, and time stands still,
As silence wraps with a gentle thrill.

Stars awaken, one by one,
As shadows dance, the day is done.
Voices echo, soft and low,
In twilight's glow, our spirits flow.

In every sigh, in every cry,
Lives a promise wrapped in the sky.
Together we merge, where silence reigns,
In voices soft, love remains.

Attunement of Spirits

In sacred spaces, souls align,
A cadence found, a love divine.
With every heartbeat, we define,
An attunement of spirits, a lifeline.

Understanding flows like a stream,
In shared glances, the softest beam.
In harmony, our hearts unite,
In every moment, pure delight.

Through trials faced, our bond grows strong,
Together navigating right and wrong.
With open arms, we find our way,
In attunement, we choose to stay.

The dance of trust, a gentle grace,
Leaves footprints in this sacred place.
In every laugh, in every tear,
Our spirits rise, strong and clear.

For in this union, we are found,
A symphony where love is crowned.
In attunement, spirits soar free,
A melody of eternity.